UNTIL
THE
KINGDOM
COMES

UNTIL THE KINGDOM COMES

POEMS

JEANNE LUTZ

*To Katherine —
Thank goodness for
beauty, all kinds of
beauty. best,
Jeanne Lutz*

atmosphere press

for Tom, with the best of my love

it is sheer joy to share Earth and an epoch with you

Volcanoes be in Sicily
And South America
I judge from my Geography —
Volcanoes nearer here
A Lava step at any time
Am I inclined to climb —
A Crater I may contemplate
Vesuvius at Home.

– Emily Dickinson, *#1705*

TABLE OF CONTENTS

SELF-PORTRAIT WITH TWINE

I once read
you are what you remember
which makes me

a man called seed
because that's what he brought
to the farm every spring
he didn't have a nose
just a deformed hole
through which he pushed
a wad of rope
and retrieved from his mouth
I was the only kid who said
do it again do it again
the rope got stuck
I stood waiting
while he all but died
to keep me entertained

I am patty the dog lady
who took out her teeth in church
and played with them
she gave them a swerving soul
of their own pretending
they were singing the hymns

I am all the lingerie I've ever worn
french lace   british silk
the soft italian gray

and I am the barn
that holy gut busting
with hay and holstein
cat   goat   pitch fork   pig
wolf spider and twine
I am that place
where yesterday I had to reach
inside a cow

3

and dig out
her dead-in-the-womb
darling

LEANING SILO OF RAPIDAN

my brothers and I bike
to the abandoned farm
because our parents tell us not to

known county-wide
for its canny slant
we marvel at the silo
leaning in the weeds
lime-salt leached
crystalized and corroded
surrounded by summer haze

defying gravity

sometimes earth and sky have no division
when we're pedaling toward heaven
me and my brothers
biking and laughing

we go off to gorenson's candy store
and leave the silo to lean alone
like a lopsided beggar
by the side of the road
like a tombstone
in the wind

NOVA'S POEM

all that summer we play
planet of the apes

and because they have the horses
my cousins get to be the apes
my brothers are the astronauts
and me I play the long-haired
mute girl named nova

the way the movie goes
astronauts land on a strange planet
ruled by brainy apes
the planet turns out to be earth
but two thousand years later
after maniacs blow it up

a talking doll and a chunk
of the statue of liberty
half buried in the beach
are all that's left of a world
the astronauts thought
would tassel forever

the way our game goes
we run through the high grass
of the meadow
the astronauts and I
until we're caught by the apes
on their horses and taken to the barn
where the astronauts are threatened
with lobotomy unless they can prove
they have some skill the apes need

the astronauts are good at sneaking
cookies and landing a hand-held radio
so the apes can listen to the ball game

me I'm good at keeping secrets

and the secret that summer
is that the apes' dad is selling
their farm to city planners

what I know that the apes don't know
is that very soon all of this will be gone
the meadow   the horses   the woods
the barn   the apple orchard
and some pleasant white hens

mute as I am let me tell you
a farm scraped away to make room
for a golf course is one kind of hurt
but there are others

we play planet of the apes
all summer long at their farm
because it is fun
and the way my brother
the one they call bright eyes screams
it's a madhouse a madhouse
is funny as hell
until one day

we're tired of being caught
escaping and being caught again
one day we refuse to run
we rise up against the apes
pelt them with rocks
hit them with sticks
the betrayal catches them by surprise
I see it in their eyes
and then it's over

from the dumb uproar of this game
of apes and astronauts fighting
from the meadow grass
where I stand mute
I watch the apes on their horses
retreating into the trees
and one riderless horse following behind
keening from its heart

7

HIS HOUSE IS FULL OF CALENDARS AND ALMANACS, CELESTIAL CHARTS AND SKY MAPS

Ah, cattails, says the hermit when she hands
    them over, follows him through the front door,
watches as he put the reeds in a jar on a stump of wood
    in the kitchen. He makes predictions about weather
and wars. The house has no electricity. He uses lanterns
    like a miner, has one real leg, one mechanical.
She sits on a paint-slobbered chair, he stands near
    the window. The girl appears as she does, full of
light and mud out of nowhere, once again
    crossing the slough and woods he thought
kept them apart. Her doing so made the slough and woods
    seem small. This is the first time she has visited
the hermit by herself. Other visits were with her father; they
    delivered liver, cake, bacon, jam jars, pickled
heart. She visits the hermit today because something
    has been going on inside her. As he watches her
watching him, he thinks about how he left Warsaw all those
    years ago, how he will never again see his family, the
Vistula River or Carpathian Mountains. In his broken-down
    overalls, stitched up shirt, he thinks about his
luck, never knowing whether it's good or bad, or how
    to reconcile the shortness of this day with the length
of his life, wondering what are all the darknesses since that
    ripe lightening when everything got lost. Is it true you
killed a man back in Poland? she asks. Expects the hermit
    to hoot, say no, that him killing someone is a local
myth, spun into rhyme, chanted on the playground for fun.
    For a laugh. But he does not laugh. Let me ask you
something, he says. Don't you think some people got it
    coming? His question does not make her afraid. She
feels her head nodding yes though does not know exactly
    why she agrees—perhaps it is because of the westerns
she watches on tv with her father, the murder mysteries she
    watches with her mother, listens as Grandma reads
Grimm's Fairy Tales. The hermit regards her. Is it true

your sins killed a priest? he asks. Yes, she says.
It's true. He looks out the window. The slough and woods,
though smaller now, are still there. Pulls up a chair,
swings his great mechanical leg, and finally, and at last, sits.

Saint Humphrey the Hermit: Beard: Contents

Saint Humphrey, c. 1660 by Salvator Rosa, Italian
Minneapolis Institute of Art

This beard with its ravines and knobs
and peaks? Its pathless woods and oak openings,
prairies and cliffs? Its hollows and ponds?

Corky white elm trees are in it,
and a young eagle eating a blue jay.
The nest of a pigeon, cursed

crowfoot, shepherd's purse, spotted
frogs hopping slopping water
along my jaw, and the eyes of a fish

perishing in its head. Snakes thick
on the hillside and wood ticks are in my beard,
a lumberman's shanty and a lumber man

in an unbecoming squat. A penciled packing list
for the trip: half-thick fur coat and pants,
compass, writing paper, twine, and spy-glass.

A separate scrap of paper giving the different
pockets in which I have placed my money,
and a meadow in which I sought and finally found

the wild apple tree with a long tap-root growing down
I declare! into the bluish-green clay of my heart.

FARE WELL

before I tell you that this is the evening
after jacob wetterling got abducted
let me tell you how my brothers and I tore through
the meal prayer without even listening to ourselves
already deep into the roast beef steaming
mashed potatoes sweet corn
fresh bread and unseparated milk
my little brother   also eleven years old
laughing with food in his mouth
suddenly
feeling our father's eyes on us

very green

very kind and soft

we set down our silverware
and asked again
the lord to bless us
and these thy gifts
for which we are about to receive
from thy bounty
through christ
our lord
amen

and mean it

and in this way learn
that our childhoods
were passing
and we were entering
the world

FUNERAL FOR A RABBIT

I wish I could
bring him back
to see what he had been
a warm diamond in the field
instead of a fist of fluff
handful of dry bone

I laid the remains out
on a white china plate
in the center of the dining room table
anointed him with cooking oil
daisy bits
lit a used candle

I invited everyone
no one came

I played the organ
sang a solo
served myself a luncheon
lemonade   sandwiches
a slice of rhubarb pie

I dug a hole near the corn crib
scooped the rabbit up
lowered him down
placed a small cross
between its unlucky paws
the cross mailed to my mother
from the reservation
after they got her donation

and while the old crows sat
choking in the trees
I filled the grave and turned away
a streak of relief lingering
an extraordinary nothing
that steadied the world

Beethoven's Ninth

animals of every denomination
                              loose in the field
dogs bark
          dogs barking deranged
                    at barn clothes on the line

me and my brothers on the hayrack
               tractor and baler snort around the land
                              mechanical animals
                         trying out for a part
                                   in the apocalypse

the train whistle   and the train
     grandma singing I wanna be   a cowboy's   sweetheart

bob dylan's subterranean
          homesick blues on the radio

                                   the cows threaten
                                   to end their lives
                                   in the slough
                    if the dogs
          come   any   closer

my brothers and I kick and bite each other
          call each other pigasaurus   spit and shove hay
                                   down
                                   each other's
                                   shirts
                    kick and bite some more
          pigasaurus

an uncle hollering
               why can't the four of you
                    be a joy to your parents
          the way your cousins are to me

13

the whole moment a kind of symphony
     in need
         of a conductor

oh   with what joy   I think about that day today

I Don't Know Why, but One Time I Lied in Confession

it was in fourth grade
I examined my conscience
memorized my list of misdeeds
made the sign of the cross
but when I asked father to bless me
all goodness wit and reason fled
phony sins poured out of my mouth

father
I told my little brother to ask dad
for a cigarette and a beer

and father
I'm the one who taught
the classroom parrot to say
bishop is a bum bishop is a bum

when the priest muttered his shock
through the confessional screen
it only encouraged me

father I said
I detest all my sins
but most of all
I am heartily sorry
for robbing gorenson's candy store
with a sawed-off air gun

that night the priest died

they found him sitting in a chair
in his room in the rectory

your sins killed father hartmann
my family teased
but they didn't know I lied

somehow on the bus and at school
everyone knew
everyone whispered
her sins killed father hartmann

everyone wanted me on their kickball team

I was glorified
horrified and mortified
I prayed I lamented
I asked mary to intercede
unable to comprehend
what it was I'm capable of
wondering what I could or could not control
through the power of lying

to this day
I don't know
but maybe we are most alive
when we're between prayers

in danger

and not sure at all

DEAD SEA SCROLL FRAGMENTS

in my school uniform I don't care
how I sit on the floor
my underwear shows

I help the nun feed the fish all the fish have movie star names
the nun is a descendant of the headless horseman

the train hollers from the west

some part of the farm is always flooded some
part of the farm is always in drought

the woods are pre-christian
full of arrow heads and ghost songs

cats are sick sick cats don't like
to be looked at when they're sick

the slough is a herd of things
it has more than one body
more than one shape more
than one smell

dogs saunter around half-heartedly
the dogs saunter nonchalant
with their red things sticking out

the train has eighty-two boxcars

the priest eternally nervous around the trappings
of anatomy worries he'll be cast out to recuperate

the train hollers to the east

cows have four parts
to their stomachs
cows suffer if they don't
get milked twice a day

dear saint agatha

don't let me suffer
like that

WHAT IS IN THE SLOUGH?

Garter snakes in a breeding ball
are in it, a dance hall for cattails,
crusty muskrat guts and what
looks like the armpit of a bear
but turns out to be Uncle Gordy's
toupee from the family reunion of '09,
a silver gilded reliquary
in the shape of a hand, a turtle
with spots on its shell that stand for
the starry sky and hoof prints following
a stampede, my favorite
boots from my favorite rain,
the memory of your ruffled hair in bed,
all the petty defeats I've ever
taken on the chin, and a hoi polloi
of frogs calling to everyone passing—
which is no one—come in, come in.

GRANDFATHER AND HIS SIMULTANEOUS EYES

one eye telescope the other microscope
one eye on the ground the other in the sky
always thinking always linking
when we walk in the woods he collects moss
because it reminds him of his childhood in bovekerke

though grandmother believes
we should be doing something
more useful than walking off every now and then
he introduces me to all his friends
meet badger he says and woodchuck
hello goldenrod you're looking very pretty

now what are these cottonwood trees
and these owl pellets about he asks

why are they here the potato bugs
the bald-faced hornets and grubs

walking stick what are you thinking

we measure the depth of the maple river
record rainfall and press
gooseneck loosestrife into an atlas

he takes my hand and says come
I want to show you where the rain goes
after it falls off our roof

we imitate grackles nuthatches and coots
like roosters we are addicted
to disturbing the peace

we count rings of fallen trees
the wrinkled leaves of a cabbage
and frozen bubbles on the icy lip
of the cow tank

these are the ways to belong to a place

and for heaven's sake he wonders
why doesn't everyone pause to adore
the connection between sunshine and rot

UNTIL THE KINGDOM COMES

the dogs are half brothers and sisters
they have the same mother
but conflicting fathers

the dogs are never allowed in the house
I see them often through the windows
and they see me

when no one is looking
I let them in
and give them bread and milk

I think of them as wayfaring strangers
in thick tawny cloaks
from some holy text

they are grateful
I almost hear them call me
samaritan

EVER SINCE BABEL RAISED ITS GLASS TO ME

The evening was beautiful on our open porch
facing the walnut trees, the slough, and the gravel road
while my Flemish mother stretched out on the old fainting couch
and drank a glass of wine. "Can I have a sip?" I whispered. Without a word
she handed over her glass. I thought there was no greater pleasure
in the world than to rest after the chores had been done, listening
as my mother did with closed eyes to the woozy frogs
and the commentary of crickets. "Will you teach me to speak Dutch?"
I asked in a murmuring, drowsy voice. "I will," she answered,
"when you're older." Her voice was serene but secluded,
and as I stretched out on the fainting couch beside her, I mused
over the bewitchment of wine and wondered how much I would taste
in the course of my life and how many lessons in Dutch I would need to take
before my time to understand would come.

MY MOTHER UPON SEEING THE PHOTO OF ME IN MY PROM DRESS

I'm wearing the dress
a semi-see-through affair
long-legged
horse-mad hips

I lie on a white and silver couch
slightly smiling
telling boys everywhere
that spring is here

the pink
that blitheness and the pose
supine vitality
sultry-lashed
mussed hair
only the devil may care
about this dress because
I sure as hell don't

mijn liefste, my mother says
the time has come
to talk of many things:
perfume and luminous skin
should your skirts cling or flare
where the hemline ought to be
whether your head has horns
or your shoulders have wings

she warns me
of all the future times I am
to be photographed
in contemplation
or in a skirt alluring and demure
with the sun behind my legs

all the future times
I will be vexed by men

who refer to me not by name
but the color of my hair

the friends of my future spouse
who, upon hearing that I'm a farmgirl,
will nudge him and say, you lucky dog

mijn schattebout, she says
luister naar mij, alstublieft :
moving is what makes you beautiful–
running with animals
brothers for playmates
beauty based on accomplishment
no adornment
no dairy princess contestant
disgracing herself in a swimsuit on stage

mijn schattebout
luister naar mij, alstublieft :
have the good sense
not to look like those girls in magazines
vamped up
theatrical
a finale without the needed
preceding moments
revealing nothing
going
nowhere

MY FATHER IN JUNE LIGHT

he loves his heart
but the heart
either works or it goes wrong

even if a better heart
were available to trade
he wouldn't want it

another heart comes with a love
of other things or worse—
indifference to what he loves
especially at the farm
where half the reason for living

possibly for all of it

is to love and be loved
by my mother
the cows
the vast uncluttered sky
fields of fresh cut hay

his concertina

his barn
his barn boots

and the train
as it muscles
along the tracks
adorned with rust
and wonder

HOME VARIATIONS

1.
who can listen unmoved
to the sweet sung love of robins?

2.
how do insects
in this short scratch called summer
hide themselves as well as they do —
baffling the rigors of the season,
safeguarding sacred eggs,
those tiny portions of ethereal heat?

3.
a swarm of bees
as big as my head
rushes a scarlet tanager
which flies away screaming

not long after I find the bird
dead on the ground

I open its caw
pick out 34 bees
and lay them on my scarf in the sun

16 return to life
lick themselves clean

imagine the story they tell their queen
after that adventure

4.
I leave strands of my hair
on a fencepost for birds to use
as nest insulation
ah and oh
the gall of me to long to be
woven into their world

56 BUCKETS OF BONDO DUST

I love the way we get lost
even with GPS
and because of GPS

I love the hand-written letters
you leave in my mailbox
even when you don't leave
a letter for weeks I don't worry
that you've run out of things to say

I love you working on my car
which I have never before confessed
because in my head I still hear
those farmer fathers like mine saying
my daughter knows
how to check the oil
jumpstart the battery and change
a tire so listen mister
you don't need to rescue her
but I do love you
working on my car

I love that some of your scars are weird
like finding gum under a table
and I love the way you sometimes sing
like your hair's on fire because sometimes it is

I love you 8 catalytic converters
14 sets of high-end snow tires
and 11 single overhead camshafts

I love how our grandfathers both
worked in the iron mines up north
the way our blood pulses
with crazy lusty peasant stock
how simpatico
purrs through our under soul

I love your wisdom and the way it descends
from some intergalactic place
I love the way you throw
percentages at people
just to halt them in their rambling

I love the way you kiss and tickle my vitals

I love that you love me
and that you loving me
makes me love this whole cockeyed world
100 tubs of tailpipes

PATTY THE DOG LADY, ON HER WAY OUT OF CHURCH, GIVES THE WORLD A PIECE OF HER MIND

I may not know
Jesus of Nazareth personally,
but I do know
Jesus of the Dollar Store,
Jesus of the Landfill,
Jesus of the Bus Stop,
Jesus of the Quarry Pit,
and Jesus
of the People Who Cheered
at the Dakota 38 Hanging
All in a Row. My Savior,
my Messiah, Jesus,
King of Government Cheese.

PATTY THE DOG LADY LOVED HER HUSBAND

he was killed in vietnam

when she got the letter she rushed off on a plane
spending three weeks at different airports
trying to find him

there were many coffins in those days
she never found him
so she claimed a body no one else claimed
naming him ernest

and bringing ernest home
she sat by him at the funeral parlor
a one-woman wake
his face grinning like a catacomb saint
in an early passionate church

she thought of the war
that wiped people out
gone the way of the dodo and the mastodon
and she wondered what final
private uprising
would fling her toward

the orbit of some invisible sun
where her motion
through the spirals
of the milky way

might drop her own corpse
back down
into the arms of a stranger
who too could choose
to mourn her
in this quiet watered room

I Love the John Deere Implement Dealer Who Loves to Love

he loves the crawl space between sun and rain
repetitive gossip of sheep in shade
and the sad last sigh of barn owl and crane

the steps he steps bounce like wagons of grain
his thoughts a bull herd keening through the glade
he loves the crawl space between sun and rain

and the nightingale whistle of the train
he loves the side of hills that never fade
and the sad last sigh of barn owl and crane

long fields of alfalfa made into chain
baled and stacked in haylofts like bars of jade
he loves the crawl space between sun and rain

his salt-lick of resentment on the wane
though mourning the heart he badly mislaid
and the sad last sigh of barn owl and crane

he's washing old songs down the milk house drain
those lush string backgrounds often softly played
he loves the crawl space between sun and rain
and the sad last sigh of barn owl and crane

BANKER DRESSED LIKE ELVIS

It is Halloween.
to get a small
improve everything,
go organic.
He has presence.
But also a pimpish
neither work-appropriate

choirboy, he is soft,
for wanting to be
you wish to see
but listen,
I can get you
at a great interest
assuming you want
You have to simplify,
your woods.
your animals.
Spray more.

Avoid all that manual
globalization's food
Borrow more money,
A farmer's job is to
be asking your animals
to only produce. No
righteous than that.
his unbuttoned shirt,
provokes me

He smiles and sings
other farmers take,
what corporations want
without listening to

recommends chickens.
as cuddly as cows,
how chickens are raised.

I'm in his office
farm loan. I want to repair,
work with the DNR,
Elvis sits, listens.
Seems polite.
overload. His costume
nor classy. Like a leering

spooky. I love you
that special snowflake
in the world and all,
Elvis says.
a big loan
rate, which you should take,
the farm to succeed.
go bigger. Clear
Drain the slough. Cage
Plow the pastures.
Buy more machinery.

labor. Get on board with
supply like they did in Brazil.
make more money.
produce. You should
and your land
need to get more
His advice, like his black wig,
plastic gold dollar-sign necklace,
with precision to the core.

about his pride in helping
in various and clever ways,
from the land
its sighs of exhaustion.
I stand up to leave. Elvis
Chickens aren't
he says. No one cares
Take out a loan for $850,000,

grow 1.2 million

an annual profit

I quell my worries
and my soul
with a wood-chopping

I get I'm not valued, I say.
but I'm happy

At this moment
in the midsummer
wrongs are righted, where
and its virtuous belongings
I don't mind sleeping
away the deer because
the fencing.

Get your hand off
my sleeve!
I feel sorry for you Elvis.

The world is healing again.
not motivated by money,
we refuse to get big,
More and more of us
small and deep and varied.
and when we say
we mean it.

chickens a year, expect to see

around $35,000. Now that is nothing
to roll your eyes at.

about the planet, humanity,
by answering him
no.

My productivity is low,
breaking even.

I still believe
night's dream where
true compassion
are restored. And
in my garden to scare
I can't afford

More and more of us are
more and more
we have no intention of getting out.
know the value of living
We are again trusting language
I love you

Somewhere There Is an Album with Photos of My Cousin Before He Became a Soldier

he talks football   kids   church
and the neck-wrenching work
at the plant
but he's really talking iraq

at night he sits
in the casino and drinks
at the poker table
he gets three of a kind
a straight
he gets nothing   he
bets   he bluffs
he wins   he loses
he watches hockey on the tv
by the pull-tab counter

he plays with a stack of chips lifting
them up letting them fall listening
to the clicking sound and the sound
of people at tables everywhere
playing with their chips

this is where his sister
at the end of her all-night
nursing shift finds him
in the casino
at the table
with a drink

she kisses his cheek and says
hey there texas hold 'em
it's time to fold 'em   let's go

she takes his car keys
and as she's buckling him in

he says what really ticks me off
are athletes who point
to the sky after scoring
and the humming he does in the car
is like birdsong in a box
iraq

MOUSE

I look at the trap by the fireplace
find the caught mouse
still alive still
fighting for its life
for time to do all the mousy things
it is that mice do

wouldn't we all fight and flail
for the chance
to be alive and living
devoting ourselves
to art and botany and languages
all kinds of languages

we study the stars
books
atlases
and sheet music
because we want more
than being
some god's spinster sister
living in an empty sea
blowing on a seashell horn

it is our right to roam
with time to be alone
and space to move about
in our surprising burdens
even the mouse wants more
than caring about hunger
or living in a meadowless room
lugging its tail
through the dust
as it runs along
the mantel
unaware
of the trap
below

TODAY WE SHEARED THE SHEEP

and I almost lost my damn mind
they are classic arcadian contentment
they're also ramshackle   wily
and rude

we're not even sure
what breed they are
but today's the day
they get sheared

and the rams acquire a brief
viking god caliber
chiseled   heroic   wise
until they get away on us

and we have to dash about shouting
at klaxon pitch to save the garden
from their ransacking hooves
and pillaging teeth

BULL OF BLUE EARTH COUNTY

I hear the farmer in her dell
singing her way toward me,
the whopping northern
shorthorn bull. For the fun of it

I plow a canyon
with my hoof. Charge
a tree. Twist
my torso, kick the boreal
out of the forest. Knock
the dipper out of the sky.
Carve my name twice
into the moon
using both horns at once:
Hadrian was here!
Hadrian was here!

She stands entranced, watching
me, this wind-cleaving
wheeling bull, her thoughts
a whispering river, my thoughts
a feral lake heat. I charge
until the tree cracks and tumbles.
I snort sweat.
Knock down every tree.
And when it rains,
I attack the rain.

"You're crazy," she says,
"but I love you."
And then dances away, leaving
me and my dilapidated dewlap
heaving beneath
the whopping empty
white mud sky.

MOMENTS BEFORE THE SPRING RAIN DROWNING OF ORLANDO, A BELOVED PIG, HE SPEAKS

I mean how different is this
than the last time?
To be the one not chosen
as part of the chosen pair
of pigs when Noah
built his ark, to know

the exact scent
of loneliness
from being awake
all night. Sure,

there's a frantic final dash
when I find myself
at the deep end of the flood.
Even the farmer in her dell
must eventually
give in to this moment. But,

it isn't bad. I feel sleepy
and I don't mind
the little dreamy curiosity
of which world I'm really in.

TOWN

when I pointed out the red lantern
I saw from the classroom window
hanging in the porch
of the beautiful woman
the priest said divert your eyes girl
divert your eyes

WHEN FIELDS AND HOURS SPAN A MILE OR TWO OR MORE

I want to kiss you I
kiss you in my mind

raindrops slide down the window
sometimes two raindrops
slide over each other and become
one sumptuous rolling one
that is the best

I imagine the hound of heaven
pursuing a soul but this time
the dog picks up
an attention span disorder
veers off to the woods
through the slough
loses the scent
forgets about souls altogether
it's more comical in my head
than it should be

you say what's so funny
I say nothing
nothing's funny

from the lack of shadow
I can tell you're gone
that is the worst

I touch the wheat with my hands
as I run through it
anyone who's heard
my heart beat knows
this is how I say
I love you

Threatened by the Possibility of Hope, My Grain Broker Throws a Bolt of Lightning First and Then Sends Me an Email

Subject: On This Morning After Elections, 2016

Oh, Ms. Farmer in your dell: Uphill begins this year. Commodity prices are dragging, weather's lousy, and the cold medication I'm taking has left me with a two-digit IQ and no feeling in my feet. I thought I could get better crop prices for you in your contract, but I was wrong. I know I should be phoning you with this news, but I'm a coward. And tired. I wish the need to work would leave me. If it did I might go to Minneapolis and look at art (in my case the *Doryphoros*, what of it). But I do need to work because Nick has been out of a job a solid year and a half, leaning on me so hard I'm feeling like a winter-bent tree. Living room's a pigsty. I'm thinking of telling him to move out, but it's hard, you know. The kids and all.

How do I fend off the twin impostors of despair and hope, my strong weakness for oxymorons, or the weight of inane cheer? How do I accept with grace the grasshopper plague that is my life? I voted for him and for that, I know you will never forgive me. I imagine when you heard that he won the election, you fell to your knees like Charlton Heston on the beach in front of the ruined Statue of Liberty. I told you. I'm a coward. I promise to fail quicker next time. Shakespeare said it better: "And, Death once dead, there's no more dying then." Until that happens, I guess I better keep going, work my tail off, sleep at any price, and leave the rest to the wind to carry grief away and bring me giddier days.

Maria

GIBBON BALLROOM

we went there to dance
almost every saturday night
we had to I swear
it was written down somewhere
like a decree from the council of trent

there were my father's friends
with their shiny music bands
donny morris
johnny helget
harold loefelmacher and the six jolly dutchmen
those lederhosen-clad yodelers
in jaeger hats with their accordions and horns

the polka the waltz
foxtrot
and the schottische

except for the waltzing
which requires elegance
the music was easy to dance to
you just hop step
twirl and laugh
in someone's arms

it was for fun

because while armies clashed in the night
the way armies do clash in the night
the pursuit of ordinary pleasure
in the gibbon ballroom
gave space to ease the inner marks
of our failures and scrub our hearts
of others' faults

we loved the long and wide stretch
of maple flooring
how giddy we felt stepping on to it

how flush our faces were
in the happy low-key glamour
in a county not oversupplied with it

but too the may-I-have-this-dance
punished shy and unsure men
women too polite to say no
and those who wanted it perfect
but waited too long

someone gutted the ballroom
turned it into a supermarket
which became a bingo parlor
that shifted into a sticky
carpeted thrift store
until someone gutted that

now it's used as a storage shed for road graders
skid steers and snow plows

but while it was the gibbon ballroom
with its roaming aromas
of hairspray and soap
cologne and smoke
floor polish and beer

where the boys did the same two steps
only faster or slower

we could be whatever we wanted to be
leaders loners knights and starlets
or villains and spies like the swivel-eyed
aunts and grannies who scrutinized
the hum of our breathlessness
as they always did
back when we were young

THE BUTCHER WHO BORROWS A PEN

in moldova
he once witnessed an execution
of rebels by a firing squad

it was a cold wet day
the rebels were allowed
umbrellas

he remembers this he says
handing me back my warmed pen
every time it rains

My Sweet Beatnik Guardian Angel

she drinks whiskey straight up
rolls her own cigarettes
eats lunch naked
teaches me how to gallop on a horse
into stampeding cattle and says
how else are you gonna grow thick skin
how else are you going to learn to howl
and mean it

take it from me she says
god is really a concoction
of red tape and a half-mad pig farmer
from bemidji
the last time I tried to talk to him
he put me on speaker phone
while he soaked in the tub
counting his mortal stars

my guardian angel
can't use chopsticks
make pie crust
or do math in her head
she's big and hairy
one quarter ape
and that's a fact jack
as she would say

she's a local angel
the same is true
of countless angels
on other farms
though to be a local anything
even an angel in blue earth county
is to miss the bus to california
or new york
where michael
raphael

and gabriel made it big
but a local angel
is something
and she's pretty good at love

CHICKEN CULLER COUSIN

she and her husband laid off
from chick-culling work
with five kids
accepted food stamps

embarrassed to use them
they drove 99 miles out of their way
in an unreliable van to another town
where they wouldn't be recognized

it was only for a couple of months
but it was bad she said until
the april sun busted through the clouds
and we found ourselves loved
in a way we did not deserve

SEASONAL AFFLICTIONS OF ENVY

he came at me like some half-dead
member of the donner party
stumbling out of the woods
longing to collapse on my porch
a welder from the manufacturing plant
a man in need of a friend

how he got here he said
was full of wrong turns
not meaning the farm
but life up to this point

how he got half-bent
was not from juggling
carbon steel
chipping knives
and solidified slag
but from

his wife having left him
for an electrician
with better health benefits
and a better back

rejection he said
returning his feet to his boots
when his son pulled up in a truck
to take him back to town
buries you like snow
effortlessly

even the well-marked
trails
remain
reliably
grim

8,000 SAINTS BALING HAY

Making hay takes two hayracks, a baler, a tractor, a hay
elevator, and as many willing people as possible to help:

the wrestling coach who doubles as a livestock auctioneer,
the butcher, Miss Mapleton, people from the bowling league,

and the Eagle Hi-Fliers 4-H club. The track coach is here,
the postal carrier, the John Deere implement dealer, and

the instructor from the vo-tech who can't stop whistling
except to explain that alfalfa came from Iran via Spain

through South America to California before finally landing
in the Midwest. Two nuns, Sister Amada Rosa and Sister

Ephigenia are here with some troubled kids from the parish.
They are given warnings about not what the machinery does

to hay and snakes, but what it will do to the unlucky kid who
falls down in front of it, which is cut you off at the ankles,

pluck your arms out of your sockets, turn you through the
steel tines, and then spit out your repackaged guts, leaving

your bones in the field to bleach in peace. This warning is not
hyperbole. It is bedrock. To make sure the kids know we're

serious, my brother holds up his hand with its two-and-a-half
missing—or remaining—fingers, depending on how you look

at it. All day, the baler gathers up the cut alfalfa and makes
hay bales with a steady *ka-chunk, ka chunk, ka-chunk,*

a mechanical heart sound in a world of happy dogs, twine
string, leather gloves, hydraulic lines, power take-offs, and

a sky lightly loaded with birds, while in the hayloft where we
stack the hay, the postal carrier plies us with old country rock

songs including "Every Rose Has Its Thorn," insisting
it's the greatest hairy rock band song ever. The comradery

and joking we do gives making hay, like early fire-tending
ancestors, a reliable warmth. From the time light swells

above the calf pens to the time we surrender to sleep, we live
in a series of exalting and terrifying fragments. I often try

to capture the reverence of it all, like the feel of cold water
going down past the Adam's apple, or the clover-scented

hope that the rain will have the decency to hold off for
a while, which it does. But no one gets a halo. There is

no get-out-of-Hell-free card, only foolish joy, and the vo-tech
instructor's whistling that's never louder than divine.

GODMOTHER IN THE KITCHEN
MASTICATING CHICKEN

there are bigger things to lose
she says
tossing
gizzard
liver
and heart
into the grinder
than a nickel
a doll's shoe
or a tooth

above us drums of thunder begin
and rain revives the longing
of whatever it falls upon
train tracks
red-winged black bird
the slough
me I want
to crawl inside his sweater
with him still in it

the woods he sings about
are not like her woods
across the road
where town people dump
their busted hot water heaters
where stuttering turkeys stutter
and dogs fornicate in the dark
his woods are light-hearted
trumpety as a stargazing lily

she snaps the neck
yanks off the wing
strips the ribcage
says there are bigger things
to pine over than boys

everything in the end is nothing
but a heap of clothes and bones

I do listen but tell her
that does not take away
from the living dew
I know he is today

LETTER TO AN ENGLISH TEACHER

because today the fields
are too wet to work
I take a walk to eagle lake
and see not an eagle

but a heron
standing on a soggy log

you would know
exactly what kind of heron it is
the latin gray this or the latin blue that
but to me

this heron is simply the color-of-rain heron

it does not seem to take
much interest in me
or what's going on in the water

it is so still
that fishermen walking by
do not point it out

the heron is a faulkner-looking bird
untidy
like a half-folded umbrella

and me
I guess I'm just another eve
who will never get it right

I left his heart
broke my own

and even though I still think the apple
is the best thing
that ever happened to women

that there is no paradise lost
only paradise turned down

it doesn't mean I don't miss it

I remember all those years ago
sitting in your classroom
looking out the window
while you read thoreau to us
in your low devoted voice
I watched the nuns
hang their laundry
those long black stockings
lifting in the wind

even now
when I am no longer
that young girl
in a fluttering dress
you'd think I'd have learned
a thing or two since then
but no

I get too close
as I always do

and the heron takes off

unhurriedly

sailing languidly east

never quite knowing
what to do
with its legs

LETTER TO WENDELL BERRY

it is still winter
not winter again but still winter
so maybe the dark mouths of the right vowels
the hips and shoulders of the best consonants
or even one sensual rune won't appear on this page
but I wanted you to know I'm trying
I've gone organic   non-GMO
the fencerows bang and jangle with rose haw and blue jays
my sheep and pigs and cows
like my fields are not numbered
but given names based on character and potential
and everywhere chickens run free

I worry though
about it not being enough
about the privilege of feeding others
the fate of nature everywhere
all the weeds I know I will not have time to pull

my mother is still dying
not transitioning passing on or crossing over but still dying
it is obscene how long dying can take
though most prayers are written to be repeated
like the shouting of territorial birds
they are never enough
you and I would not let animals suffer like that

what will I plant in her deep bare garden?

I wish my farm could be the perfect farm
with just the right amount of amish intuition and grace
I wish our country was a perfect country
with the right amount of gandhi and good will
and I want on some future winter day to look back and say
that my life has been one beautiful rampage
that took place in a mystical place
not the mystical on bended knee kind of mystical

but something like when you know
you're the only mortal
in the forest

WHY DOES MY FATHER LOVE TO WATCH THOSE OLD WESTERNS ANYWAY?

it's not the saloon
with its piano player
five card stud
painted ladies in frothy petticoats
the harmless brawling
the bounty hunters stopping
by to buy themselves
two fingers of red eye
or the toothless codger waving
his nugget of gold

is it then the sense of private justice?

the semi-nomadic
cowboy wandering
from place to place
fed up
with what ain't right
bringing him to his senses
then to his gun
fighting outlaws
falling for women
and then back to his senses again
sleeping alone by the fire
while a coyote communes
with the moon beyond
the purple hills
or is simply that
being on a horse
levels the playing field

on a horse everyone
is strong and fast

and free

TAPER VS. FADE

Before we go to sit with my mother in hospice,
I pick up the scissors to cut my father's hair,
he and his weather-busted heart sunk hunched
into the viscera of his lift chair,
trusting, subdued, waiting for me to begin.
His walker where he can reach it.

The truth is, I can't cut it. I mean I can't get the scissors
and comb lined up while I hold long stretches
of his hair—the color of apparitions—between
my fingers. I can't wield these stupid barber shears —
            I'm left-handed and sobbing
like a concertina. I cannot do this thing, this doing

what my mother has always done, which is cut
my father's hair, his beautiful, thick hair, now like shrieks
climbing up the side of his head. The more I try
            to fix it, the more it looks
as if I am helping him blend his way onto the film set
of *The Cabinet of Dr. Caligari*—a world of serrated
landscapes, sharp angles, tilted windows
and walls, staircases clamoring discordant diagonals. Trees
            with stabby leaves. Knives for grass.

I give him a mirror and he starts laughing—not over
the German Expressionist haircut, I realize, but at
some memory in his head. Laughing, he tells a story

from when he was young, long-haired and hitchhiking.
He got picked up in a van driven by nuns. They gave him
a crew cut and then dropped him off at the YMCA. Cutting
his hair becomes funny to me, too, because suddenly I get it:
the intimacy of a daughter caring for her father in old age
is not a good place for us to go for pictures of an ideal life,

but here we are together, and that's exactly why we go.

A To-Do List Left Behind for My Napping Father

✓ soak your teeth

✓ wear compression socks

✓ draw self-portraits even though you will never be good at hair

✓ pretend to smoke a pipe and stare whenever someone says something important

✓ refuse to let your heart beat like a medieval world encrusted with superstition

✓ cavort like a racing horse with a sabotaged bridle still winning some world cup

✓ invite birds to make a rookery of your eyebrows

✓ sing like the eye of a whooper swan untouched by mortals

✓ travel at the speed of light on the back of every condor

✓ outsoar me

✓ see me as if through sweeter air

AFTER ANOTHER SHOOTING IN THE NEWS

holsteins are shapes in the dark
not black and white
the shapes change
when bodies collide
heads blunt like
sheer cliffs

they chew their cud
belch
always lowing
roaming
the dung-turned-to-dirt earth
their thoughts plain
and sparse

but now it's time for me
to go back up to the house

I say farewell to them
to the fling
and swipe of their tails

in my leaving
I am overcome
by perfect despair
overcome by my leaving
I mourn the things
beyond them
mourn even more
the things beyond me

WE HAVE ART, NIETZSCHE SAID, SO THAT WE SHALL NOT BE DESTROYED BY THE TRUTH

The first time Frank called me
it was to say he wanted to buy my land
and began unfurling his plans

to start a canine center, a dog track
and an indoor water park.
You wouldn't think, he said,
that water parks are a gold mine,
but waters parks are a gold mine,
look at Wisconsin Dells—you
ever been to Wisconsin Dells?
See, so you know. That's where
the professional athletes
and their kids all go.

Frank could have been an NBA player
if it weren't for his frigging heart.
He could do a left-handed layup,
make a basket from downtown.

He wanted to build
some other kind of theme park, too—
not sure what yet. He lived in
and worked out of his RV—
debt-free, thank God.

I'm just like everyone else around here, he said.
I work. I've always worked, and if I didn't,
Pops got the belt out and beat my butt.

I'm not afraid of anything, Frank said.

It was the second time he called—not
to pressure me, well maybe a little,
but really just to talk so I just listened:

Say I got into a fight with a shark, Frank said.
Sure, I might end up with a colonoscopy bag
or whatever, but I'd fight a shark. I'd say,
bring it on, shark.

Yeah, Pops was a yeller,
user of the f word,
and loved gas station beef jerky.
He died just after the Soviet Union did.
I swear I didn't see it coming, Frank said.

Yelling is the mark of an emperor,
the self-crowning kind.

Someone who can't tell the difference
between love
and war.

potholes

walls

people

we keep running into them

why is there something rather than nothing?

why this skin prickling in mortal expectation
this leading me to your bed
this hip's tilt
this sad
sad
dumbly eloquent
heart in your hand?

why isn't the world better than it is?

what is the ache
within an ache?

what do we really want
when we love the trees
or picking apples with our mothers?

what is the something
that doesn't ever get solved
in being human?

The third time Frank called
he said through bites of apple,
It'll be done the right way
once I buy your land.

I'll dig up all the fieldstones—
it'll cost a couple of g's—sheesh!
there must be 99 thousand rocks
in your fields—
rocks, mud and flies—
how do you people live like that?

He said, I'll hire five hundred people
and grease the politicians. They'll say,
Oh Frank! I know him.
Frankie owns Blue Earth County.
I wanna do business with Frank.
Or whatever. I'll say
to the politicians here what I said
to the politicians in Duluth:
Guys, I got a hypersonic jet in Winnipeg.
What do you got around here for an airstrip?
Politicians can hook you up with movers
you don't know how to shake.

I am surrounded by feedlots cafos algae bloom
global farmers entrenched in the status quo
they call me *interesting*
I just want to be alone

there are things
I want to talk about with Frank
but can't

how we're still only half awake
in a fake republic

how we have conjured away
our history through
bullet   ballot
slashing   burning
not to mention
bullying the world
as if humans were only
one animal among many

our lamentable habit
of loving too late

I want to say to Frank
pollution has made our skies
shabby   drab everywhere
for centuries to come

our eyes once knew a depth of blue
now only found
in literature   art
with our eyes closed
in our dreams

we are shaped by our circumstances
and our landscapes

I am minnesota river valley
my creeds come from here
my word choices
my philosophies
my ideas of beauty
my barbaric yawp

if you are the unsure type
or into marketing
or you just like stability
I'll tell you right now
I don't fit into any one box
my limbs are too long
what's more
I have irreconcilable differences
that's what I get for growing up
in a tornado belt

I'm from where the weather doesn't care
if you're walking with a prosthetic
what you owe the bank
how many miles you get to the gallon
or if you're turned inside out
and hanging
with your heart
dangling
though attached

work is my destiny
everything else is just showing off

I love my body rising
with friskiness and heat
I'll love you frontwards
and backwards
or in the middle
of some equinox storm

though mine eyes have seen the glory
I follow my own vision

I believe in
blue earth
mystery
gravel roads
baling hay and saints
holy water and sweet corn
love all love divine
hopping trains
the clarinet polka
may day
and newborn anything

This is the question we live with:
how do we find beauty in a broken world?
The terror in our own families, it's daily.

Can we at least be honest,
skillfully and gracefully honest?
Let us give each other our word
that we will be honest because
what we are all up against is cliché.
We stereotype those
with whom we don't agree,
media outlets stereotype us all,
but we are families.
These are our relationships.

I am shaped by North Country,
6,500 rivers, 11,000 lakes,
year-round weather,
and the American farm family I grew up in.
There is always a flurry at the door,
the swish of thrown-off chore clothes.
We have family suppers,
large family suppers,
and no one agrees.
We are direct.
How to make peace
with our conflicts?

There have been many deaths
in my family, as there have been
in other families. How do we
find beauty in death?

Let us begin by acknowledging
the inexpressible pain of parting

and then let us find refuge
in change, and in what endures—
the four seasons,
the waning
and waxing
of the moon,
our eternal, inner beings.

We are resilient.
We adapt.
Through change,
we grow.

Conversations can be engines for change, but it is difficult. Sometimes the room grows crowded with risky hanging slabs of dialogue. Locutions bent and heaved. Meals finished in gists. Piths. The crooked elegance with which we try to stick them in.

I watch BBC, listen to NPR, and read the *New York Times*. An aunt refuses to watch Fox News because it's too liberal. She wants to know how her son, who moved to Buenos Aires, can use the pronouns they, them, we, and us. *I don't understand*, she says. *Help me understand.*

Our response to catastrophe is often bewilderment, whether in families or across entire countries. Covid glides in on owl's wings during a vulnerable time in America. Science and wearing masks become political. The president dares the virus to touch him, like Lear raging against the storm.

More than one niece refuses to eat meat.

Scenes of eruption—Pompeii, Herculaneum, Krakatoa—recur, buckled lips, contractions of syntax, collapsed nouns, the lacerations our dashes inflict. In the absence of the ordinary sutures of language, tranquility vanishes. Ellipses prevail.

I love my slough of brothers, cousins, aunts, uncles, and in-laws. But we can't honestly know how Native American farmers feel, I say, or how Black farmers, Brown farmers, or how Hmong farmers feel. We don't know. Empathy fatigue may be a thing, it is also a privilege. *There's that word again—privilege.* Family members walk out. I'm sorry, but this is where we are. Maybe we'll talk again tomorrow. Maybe we won't. I know they feel badly. I feel badly.

How do we do it? How do we keep talking? Maybe we don't have the words, the scholarly vocabulary, or elegant persuasion skills of great orators past, maybe we just don't want to get into it. I don't know how to do this. I just know we shouldn't give up.

Let us embrace, like Gertrude Stein, what it feels like
to stand in the vitality of struggle. Let us think of dignity,
kindness, harmony, safekeeping, tenderness and joy
as a matter of will once the egos are shed. And while
we're at it, let us praise Gwen Westerman, Rachel Carson, Louise
Erdrich, and Terry Tempest Williams, for they are good.
It is right to give them thanks and praise.

Let us embrace hope. Otherwise, I don't think we can go on.

Nature teaches all. Some animals
will come right up to you. They have no fear.
What would that be like if there wasn't any fear?

Beauty can bind us all.

Beauty in nature is the origin of awe and wonder.
Just once, give animals the right-of-way. Stop whatever it is
you're driving. Get out of your seat. Bow.

Earth has a pulse. It registers all: drones, robins, rising pine,
beetles in a scurry, the shed skin of snakes, every human voice.
Scientists with their seismometers proclaim
what indigenous wisdom has always known: Earth is alive.
It is our turn to listen, honor, and behave on the land we call
home.

the old deed to my land is haptic
I can feel the print with my fingers
I cannot bring myself to burn it
instead I commit the world as it is to the flame
and commit that to the soil
I commit to the ring of life linking me
to the dead
and the not-yet living

to ~~the god I was given~~ Mother Earth:

please look to this place
from which my farm flows
to the iron of spilled blood in the loam
look to me
to those I have wronged
to those who have wronged me
help me farm for tomorrow
restitute for yesterday
and work for a blue sky
I hope my babies will live to see

The last time I talked to Frank
he came at me all nostril and horn:

What do you mean you
don't want to sell your land to me?
You haven't even heard
my other theme park idea yet.

Frank and I were sitting in Bakers Square.
He scraped off the whipped cream
from his French silk pie.

You ever been to Universal Studios? he asked.
They recreated dinosaurs freaking out over earthquakes,
lava and whatever running down their legs
because of the frigging volcanoes,
which got me thinking, I'm gonna dig
a bunch of trenches and I'm going
to teach people what their great-grandparents

or their great great-grandparents went through
during World War One:
trench warfare and shell shock, so when you
go down into the trenches, it's gonna feel like
you're being attacked. I'm talking bombs,
cannons, tanks, mustard gas—
and it'll feel real, trust me
because the trenches will be shaking,
and then
there's going to be a laser light show.
I can't believe you're saying no to this.

In the end
Frank ate the scraped-off
whipped cream anyway.

He said, I think Pops
would have liked my idea, too.

I still always kinda miss him.

BOILING UP NEWSPAPERS TO MAKE RELIEF MAPS OUT OF PAPIER-MÂCHÉ

everything we do
freud said
is autobiographical

what we make
what we wreck
why we paint beasts

and birds
we have never seen
who it is we gravitate to

why we cannot forget

you kissed me at the neck
and at the waist
you took my ear in your teeth

thunderstorms at night
make me jump
like a nervous horse

thunder rattles the walls
the stanchions in the barn
cattails in the ditch

reminding me
how we carry
within us

for all of our lives
the hidden presence
of others

sounds we've heard and learned
by heart to recall as we stumble
down the broken road of memory

your presence remains
within me everyday
in all of my rattling

over every land I ride

Lost in Darwin

it is that kind of town
to just go slack and empty
to be nobodies in particular
and by that notion
more specifically ourselves
where the world's largest ball of twine
sits permanently parked
beneath the water tower
twine made from the same roughage we are
animal gut
volcanic ash
and the marzipany murk of the lake

who could have imagined
an infinite thing
called possibility

for every crash
there's a near miss
for every failed ceremony
a party

but it's not even breakfast time yet

he parks his truck next to the water tower
and we listen to the world's
largest ball of twine
surge
sigh
and rampage
behaving like our itches and wishes
careening in some third stanza
and then grows mute
it symbolizes them
mirrors them
freeing us at last
from the inaccuracy
of words

GODFATHER

on the day of my visit I tell him
about the train that ran off the tracks
how it gashed and badgered his pasture
I don't want to be here I'm not CNN
I have no other news

which doesn't matter

he's on medication and not himself
his nose and arms full of tubes
a monitor hitched to his heart
and when the nurse comes in
he thinks she's a raccoon and tells her
to get the hell out of his corn

he wants to yank everything out
and though I don't know how to be here
I hold his hands I tell him
when you get out of here
there will be hot beef sandwiches
and cake some really good cake I tell him

you can say hello again to the chicken coop
the hedges and the windmill
pails buckets and all that machinery in the shed
your dogs will bark pomp
and your dogs will bark circumstance
there will be fishing some really good fishing
and commodity prices on the rise

he stops bucking and pulling at the tubes

what I really want to know he says
is what did the train do next
did it run out of steam did it turn to miss
my cows the nosy heifer bastards
or did it laugh and fly
like a dragon in the rain

JOAN OF ARC'S INSTRUCTIONS FOR THE SOUL URGE

leave the mud on
perfect your sense of direction
throw dead tractors over cliffs
ring that bell like it's dinnertime

be true as raw meat
use udder balm to keep your feet soft
always carry a straight slot and pliers
never plow the same field twice

know that some people want you
to stay the same but tell them
you are not breakfast cereal
at least you better not be

when the cornfield starts curling
and the crows get too many
drive through town shouting
we're all going to live forever

work eighteen-hour days
no need to walk the line
just learn to look at metal
and melt it with your eyes

IN GOOD THUNDER FOR A FAMILY
WEDDING WHERE THE GROOM SINGS
PURPLE RAIN TO HIS BRIDE

He sings with a heartfelt I-don't-know-what, wringing
screeches, his eyes closed, his feet half-tapping. Despite
swooning good looks, he has always been unlucky in love

yet here he is singing a Black man's song
in a tiny White town named after a Dakota leader
about how he never meant to cause her any problems,

about how he only wants to see her laughing,
which gives piquancy to this moment. It is after all,
his fourth marriage, to a hairdresser two decades

younger. He sings as if begging a blessing —
from God, the church, from us, from his new bride's
ex-boyfriends with their apps, tattoos, and beards,

and his new bride, who he will no doubt annoy and fail
in a thousand different ways, a thousand different times.
He's up there now singing his heart and his guts out

like a cat caught on a barbed wire fence
while the priest and the altar boys sweat and shift
in their long, outdated robes. Everyone watching

and listening, just watching and listening. There's no time
to think that he's singing well or badly, even when
he forgets the lines and warbles off-key.

When the last word is done, our applause roars
to a crescendo, all of us in good clothes,
who would never stand up like that or sing like that,

not in a thousand years, let alone believe in marriage again
over and over and over and over, so stupidly, so beautiful,
none of us, in good clothes, sitting in the pews.

LOVE POEM FOR THE END TIMES

ice cubes in glasses shine next to our legs
as we sit on the stoop of the barn
in the tenderloin heat of this meaty july

our pulped-out lemonade long gone

we want to shed our clothes
but the world has changed
too much for us
to do as we please

instead
we sit in the sun listening
to the slow white drawl
of ice cubes on the wane

I read somewhere that earth will spin faster
as the polar caps thaw
and when all the glaciers melt
michael phelps will rule the world

seriously though
if the world really does end
not by way of fire
but another great flood,
well I'd just have to have
my way with you that's all,
mad and frantic
one last time
right here in the water
—I'm talking undomesticated
aqua erotica
while all the world's hermits
and snakes and bankers float by

then you and I will disappear
like so many glittering cities,

sinking into our own separate heavens,
little cubes of glaciers
spinning in our mouths
as we go

THE TIME MY UNCLE TOOK ME FISHING

the idea is to balance yourself in a boat
hold something in your hand
look off into the distance
and talk about life

he's a giant man   a self-made good man
with a head bigger than a horse
and a voice that sounds like he was born old
born smoking   born drinking scotch
still talking into a rotary phone
with fists as big as russian kettlebells
and the kind of pale eyes
that blind prophets had in ancient greece

all afternoon we catch nothing
which is embarrassing for him

it gets to the point where he buys fish
from fishermen in a passing boat
which is humiliating

we are sunburnt

seasick

beauty is everywhere he says
keep your words soft and sweet
in case you have to eat them
and remember
the truth doesn't fit
on a bumper sticker

I'm a kid
I hang on to his words
in a way adults never do
his voice a smashed fog horn
but a voice that would sing lullabies
to someone who is dying

or leaving forever
or growing up too fast

and in the distance
still more distance

SHOULD I FALL OUT OF AN AIRPLANE AND SHOULD SOME AMISH FARMER FIND ME

I want to die beyond comprehension
I want people to say wow
how did she get here
why is she like that
think of the mystical possibilities
of being found naked dead
in the middle of a field of hay
like an invulnerable goddess

ACKNOWLEDGMENTS

Grateful acknowledgment is made to the editors of the following periodicals and venues where these poems first appeared, some in slightly different versions and under different titles:

Autonatta: "Godfather"

Conduit: "Dead Sea Scroll Fragments"

KAXE Radio Station:
"Should I Fall out of an Airplane and Should Some Amish Farmer Find Me"

Magnolia Review:
"In Good Thunder for a Family Wedding Where the Groom Sings Purple Rain to His Bride"
"Lost in Darwin"
"Nova's Poem"
"Taper vs. Fade"

Midway Journal:
"Moments Before the Spring Rain Drowning of Orlando, a Beloved Pig He Speaks"
"8,000 Saints Baling Hay"

Poetry City, USA: "The Butcher Who Borrows a Pen"

Shot Glass Journal: "What Is in the Slough?"

Still Point Arts Quarterly: "Gibbon Ballroom"

The Hopper Literary Magazine: "Home Variations"

The Missouri Review:
"Self-Portrait with Twine"
"Grandfather and His Simultaneous Eyes"
"Letter to an English Teacher"
"Letter to Wendell Berry" (nominated for a Pushcart Prize)
"The Time My Uncle Took Me Fishing"

The Moccasin: "Fare Well"

Tinderbox Poetry Journal: "Joan of Arc's Instructions for the Soul Urge"

Whistling Shade: "I Love the John Deere Implement Dealer Who Loves to Love"

Winning Writers: "We Have Art, Nietzsche Said, so That We Shall Not Be Destroyed by the Truth"

Many people contributed to this book in one way or another. I want to especially thank those who actively went over the manuscript: Trista Edwards, editor extraordinaire at Atmosphere Press, Deborah Keenan, Lee Kisling, Katherine Rauk, Carolyn Williams-Noren, Brett Elizabeth Jenkins, Molly Sutton Kiefer, Jonathan Proctor, and Todd Boss. Thank you to Ronaldo Alves, Nick Courtright, Alex Kale, Erin Larson, and Evan Courtright, also of Atmosphere Press, for making my book beautiful and for your endless enthusiasm.

Thank you to the other winners with me during our year-long Loft Mentor Fellowship writers series: Sagirah Shahid, Michael Kleber-Diggs, Gabriella Anais Deal-Marquez, Isela Gomez, Elizabeth Horneber, Jody Lulich, Glenda Reed, James Stephenson, Kasey Payette, Lynda McDonnell, and Beth Mayer. Thank you thank you THANK YOU to our mentors Sherry Quan Lee, Sean Hill, Carolyn Holbrook, Marisha Chamberlain, Joni Tevis, Cristina Henriquez, and the goddess Sherrie Fernandez-Williams. Your patience, wisdom, and grace are more than I deserve.

I remain in deep appreciation for the Oberholtzer Foundation and its residency program: for three summers in a row I was lucky enough to share Mallard Island and its 30,000 books with some other poets who remain like beautiful-hearted sisters to me: Athena Kildegaard, Paula Cisewski, Francine Sterle, Elizabeth Tannen, Kara Olson, Nancy Shih-Knodel, Jasmin Rae Ziegler, and again, Katherine Rauk, Brett Elizabeth Jenkins, and Carolyn Williams-Noren. Thank you Don Jones and Grandmother Drum. Rave on!

Thank you to the people of Cracked Walnut and our annual Traveling LitFest, especially Mary Schmidt and David Stein. I remain humbled to have served on the board working with people committed to creating spaces for the diverse voices wanting and needing to be heard. I remain proud of the anthologies that ensued: *Thresholds* and *After the Equinox*. Rave on!

Thank you to the people who asked me to get up in front of their microphones: the Literary Bridges Reading series with Donna Isaac and Stanley Kusunoki, the Minneapolis TV Network and Ronald Palmer, Literary Death Match and Adrian Todd Zuniga, Poets and Pints and David Bayliss, Writers Resist, Troubadour's, 555, Maeve's Sessions, St. Sophia's Church in Stockholm, the Phipps Center for the Arts in Hudson and the Octopus Literary Salon in Oakland. Thank you to 2001: A Space, Artista Bottega, Coffee Hag, the Minneapolis Institute of Art, Rogue Buddha Art Gallery and Nicholas Harper for letting me host readings in your beautiful places. Rave on!

Thank you to editor Jim Rogers for including my work in the anthology, *Broad Wings, Long Legs: A Rookery of Heron Poems*. And thank you to editors Margaret Hasse and Athena Kildegaard for including my poems in the anthology *Rocked by the Waters: Poems on Motherhood*. Rave on!

I remain in deep appreciation for the support of the National Endowment for the Arts, the Jerome Foundation, the Loft Literary Center, and the Minnesota Center for Book Arts. Thank you League of Minnesota Poets and Peter Stein, the Southern Minnesota Poets Society, Derek Liebertz and Yvonne Cariveau. Thank you to the Clean Water and Land Legacy Amendment, the Minnesota State Arts Board, Lina Belar, and the Green Island Preserve. Rave on! Rave on! Rave on!

Thank you to those who told me to take my writing seriously: Jonis Agee, Jim Heynen, Michael Gorman, Barton Sutter, Alex Pate, Mary Carroll Moore, Mechelle Avey, Ellen Hart, Carol Bly, Marion Gomez, Jude Nutter, Thomas R. Smith, Ethna McKiernan, and Danez Smith.

Thank you to English teachers everywhere, especially the good ones, especially my high school English teacher, Mr. Thiem. I wish you could have taught my babies.

Above all, thank you to my family: my husband, our sons, my pile of brothers, in-laws, grandparents, godparents, uncles and aunts, my nieces, my nephews, my 66 first cousins, those who remain farmers, and everyone in the next generation who have gone on to Perdue, University of Minnesota, American University of Dubai, University of Wisconsin, Iowa State, National Taiwan University, Georgia State, Life University, Simmons University, Dunwoody,

Clark University, University of St. Thomas, Harvard, Waseca Vo-tech, University of North Dakota, University of Washington, Minnesota State, Winona State University, Mankato Vo-tech, Northwestern College, University of Chicago, Columbia Law, Oxford, Middlebury, Yale, Complutense University of Madrid, Duke, and Cornell to become web app engineers, artists, art historians, chiropractors, athletic trainers, teachers, mechanics, CEOs, masons, roofers, social services directors, registered nurses, graphic designers, athletes, psychiatrists, carpenters, financial advisors, occupational therapists, accountants, dental hygienists, lawyers, firemen, doctors, welders, choreographers, elderly care workers, electricians, and Peace Corps volunteers while learning Chinese, German, Arabic, French, Korean, Afaan Oromoo, Spanish, Latin, Japanese, Italian, Turkish, Quechua, Danish, and Dutch languages along the way. Mom and Dad, I miss you.

ABOUT THE AUTHOR

Jeanne Lutz grew up on a small dairy farm in southern Minnesota, attended the National University of Ireland Galway, and spent two years in Japan. In addition to having her poetry supported by the National Endowment for the Arts, the Jerome Foundation, the Oberholtzer Foundation, and the Minnesota Center for Book Arts, she is a Pushcart Prize nominee, Best-of-the-Net nominee, and winner of the Loft Mentor Series for poetry. Jeanne divides her time between the family farm, giving tours at the Minneapolis Institute of Art, and researching agrarian stewardship in Italy.

Visit her online at **jeannelutz.com**

Made in the USA
Monee, IL
16 February 2022